HOORAY HENRY

Annie Tempest

MULLER, BLOND & WHITE

First published in Great Britain in 1986 by Muller, Blond & White Limited,
55 Great Ormond Street, London WC1N 3HZ

British Library Cataloguing in Publication Data

Tempest, Annie
Hooray Henry.
1. English wit and humor, Pictorial
I. Title
74.5'942   NC1479

ISBN 0-584-11146-0

Printed and bound in Great Britain by
R. J. Acford, Chichester, Sussex

To P.A.F.

A special thanks to Sue Macartney-Snape,
for her advice and encouragement throughout
the making of this book.

HOORAY HENRY

HABITAT   Battersea, Fulham, parts of Stockwell, Kennington and Clapham.

WEEKENDS   Not fussy providing it's a stately pile 2-8 hours on motorway.

UNIFORM   Barbour and/or Husky, flat hat, wellies (see *How Green Are Your . . .* also by Annie Tempest).

ABROAD   Not too good at this, though mind-narrowing travels in coveys to the slopes are obligatory.

CHIN   Less.

MOUTH   Highly elastic rosebud.

NOSE   Generally long, sharp and airborne though often Wellingtonian in ageing thoroughbreds.

MAGAZINES   *Tatler, Harpers & Queen, Private Eye, Farmers Weekly* (has been *told* to read *The Spectator*).

WIVES   By arrangement, preferably with grouse moors and Cordon Bleu diploma: Henrietta, Sarah, Emma, Camilla.

CALENDAR

June 4th*	Fourth of June	*May 29th this year.
August 12th	Grouse	
September 1st	Partridge	
October 1st	Pheasant	

A BIRD IN BURKES IS WORTH TWO IN THE TELEPHONE DIRECTORY

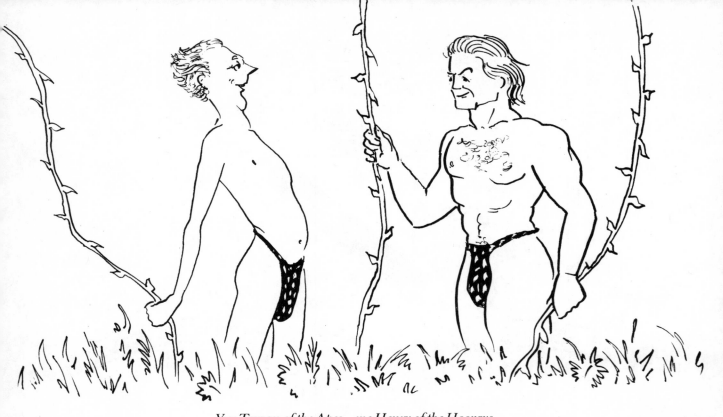

You Tarzan of the Apes — me Henry of the Hoorays.

Forceps, doctor. The silver spoon's jammed.

I want port! Give me port!

He hasn't stopped crying since I told him he was a second son.

Now stop crib-biting, Miss Sophie.

Homo Purdiens also migrates north around the 12th August.

We're hoping that when she grows up she'll marry a grouse moor.

Such luck! He bears an uncanny resemblance to his ducal great grandparent.

Is that wisteria you've got growing up your legs?

Bows? On tennis shoes?

That's a funny place for a piggy bank, Master Hamish.

DARling — what have you done? You look divine.

Shoulders back, Filofax forward.

Don't jump! It's been found!
Your Filofax has been found!

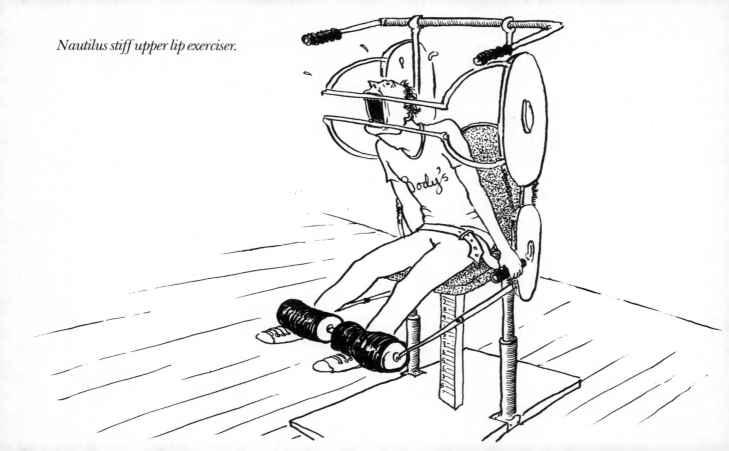

Nautilus stiff upper lip exerciser.

Snap.

She's the type Father would like

   but not the sort one could take home to Mother.

Tell me, if you don't hunt, shoot or fish, what <u>do</u> you do?

A pint of gin and tonic in a straight glass for the lady.

Gossip Column.

A Very High Hen.

I thought smack was something nannies did.

I don't know what we'd do without Jean-Marc, he whips up the most aerodynamic bread rolls.

Yes! And who the Fucky-Wucky's that?

Hello is that Debsy-Websy?

Are you there Moriarty?

It's either some new disease or the skiing season's here again.

She's got the bit between her teeth.

Don't you recognise an In Joke when your hear one?

I think he's a farmer — he told me he was off to sow some wild oats.

Oughtn't you to mingle darling?

Darling, where <u>did</u> you get your sense of humour? Your parents don't seem to have one.

Eternal Gate Crashers.

These could be our Mr Rights.

I sentence you to three months in the gossip columns.

But Ma, he's frightfully well connected. He knows the Duke of Ellington.

Hugo's latest claim to fame is that his family can be traced back to the dinosaurs.

I thought it was <u>me</u> who was supposed to lie back and think of England.

Right! Now all I have to do is find myself a husband.

Darling, would you get the jar of maggots from my morning suit pocket?

Drawing room, darling. I'm going to have my port.

You must be Henry's old trout.

So kind of you to put me up for such a marvellous six months.

When you're in England I'm sure Mama would love to have you to tea.

Despite my family being in the regiment for generations they still won't take me with flat feet.

. . . and here we have the famous Swingeing-Bigot Titian — believed to be . . .

There must be __some__ way of linking up this leak to the hot water system.

This little lot should out-do Magnolia Fess-Point's hardware at the charity meeting.

I simply can't understand why the commies don't want to live like us.

It's the Lord's coat of arms, only experts aren't sure whether it's a bagel or a halo.

Fleurs-de-lys are trumps.

She's becoming more like a horse every day. I'm positive I saw her ears go back.

I reckon she needs a martingale.

. . . and when you've finished Benson, you can do my sit-ups too.

The only snag will be sharing Heaven with Guardian readers.

I always like to look my best when hunting with the Quorn.

Perfect for a trout fly! May I take a cutting?

Psst, wanna buy a hot fishing rod, with a couple of salmon flies thrown in?

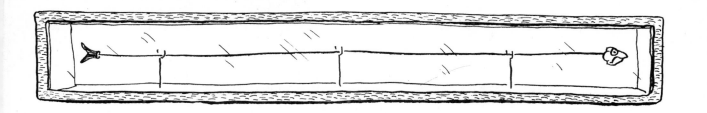

We ate the bit in the middle.

Admiral Codrington. Mmm, wasn't he River Plate 1934?

14 Golf GTI's, 2 BMW 323i's and 7 Range Rovers . . .

Perhaps you'd like to borrow Henry's Fly-mo?

Lord and Lady Fothersbotham.

I can see First and Second class but where's Upper class?

'. . . speaking as the average upper-class twit in the street . . .'

The Glorious Twelfth.

Hordes of them troupe past with packs
on their backs every day...

Afternoon! Afternoon!

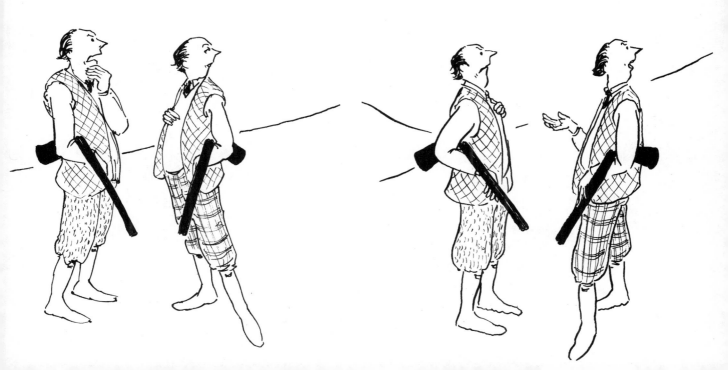

Woopsie!

Driven Grouse.

You damn near shot my wife!

Awfully sorry, old chap — maybe you'd like a crack at mine?

That's awfully kind of you, Brigadier.

Drag Hound.

No, no! There's obviously been a ghastly mistake — my parents put me down for Eton and <u>Heaven</u> at birth.